ALTERNATOR
BOOKS™

# SOUND AND LIGHT WAVES

## INVESTIGATIONS

KAREN LATCHANA KENNEY

To our future scientists and their unknown discoveries

Content Consultant: Dr. Neal D. Clements, Professional Engineer

Lerner Publications Company
A division of Lerner Publishing Group, Inc.
241 First Avenue North
Minneapolis, MN 55401 USA

For reading levels and more information, look up this title at www.lernerbooks.com.

Main body text set in Aptifer Slab Regular 11.5/18.
Typeface provided by Linotype AG.


**Library of Congress Cataloging-in-Publication Data**

Names: Kenney, Karen Latchana.
Title: Sound and light waves investigations / by Karen Latchana Kenney.
Description: Minneapolis: Lerner Publications, Alternator Books, [2018] | Series: Key questions in physical science | Audience: Age 8–12. | Audience: Grade 4 to 6. | Includes bibliographical references and index.
Identifiers: LCCN 2016049277 (print) | LCCN 2016050370 (ebook) | ISBN 9781512440041 (lb : alk. paper) | ISBN 9781512449594 (eb pdf)
Subjects: LCSH: Sound-waves—Juvenile literature. | Wave theory of light—Juvenile literature. | Sound—Juvenile literature. | Light—Juvenile literature. | Wave-motion, Theory of—Juvenile literature.
Classification: LCC QC243.2 .K46 2018 (print) | LCC QC243.2 (ebook) | DDC 534—dc23

LC record available at https://lccn.loc.gov/2016049277

Manufactured in the United States of America
1-42266-26123-3/21/2017

# CONTENTS

# STREET BEATS

**C**an you hear it? It's your favorite band playing at a concert. The music gets louder and louder the closer you get to the stage. In the crowd, everyone's dancing. You can all feel the beat. The low bass is pounding in your chest. The stage lights switch from red to yellow and blue. A spotlight follows the lead singer. Flashing lights highlight

You can feel a song's low bass notes in your body, but not the higher notes. That is because sound travels in waves. The low notes have longer waves that move more slowly. So you can feel them as they travel through your body!

Sound and light waves make a concert loud and exciting.

the beat. Their light travels in waves. You don't feel the light waves, but they help you see everything around you.

Ever wonder why low sounds make your body vibrate? Or why a leaf is green? Or even how bats can fly in the dark? Scientists ask these kinds of questions as they study the world and wonder how it works. They test their theories and come up with answers based on their evidence. This is known as scientific inquiry. What questions do you have about sound and light?

# CHAPTER 1

# HOW DOES LIGHT TRAVEL?

**H**ave you ever done the wave at a football game? One section of the crowd stands up waving their arms. They sit down, and then the next section does it. The movement travels from one part of the stadium to the next.

The crowd's wave starts at a source. That's where the energy is most intense. From there the energy spreads. Sound and light travel in a way that is similar to the crowd's wave at a football game. They are forms of energy that move in waves from a source. Their energy spreads out from a source in all directions.

Fans at a sports stadium demonstrate the basic properties of sound and light waves.

Although we cannot see waves in light, scientists observed other waves in nature for clues about the nature of light. Thomas Young's observations of the waves in water inspired him to hypothesize about how light waves travel.

## TRANSVERSE WAVES

Have you seen a duck rising and falling as it floats on the water? The duck moves with the water's waves as they travel to the shore. This type of wave is known as a **transverse wave**, a wave that travels in a perpendicular direction along its path. The high point of this kind of wave—the part where the duck bobs up in the water—is called the crest. The low point, where the duck dips down, is the trough.

In the early nineteenth century, British doctor Thomas Young used his observations of transverse waves in water to help him determine how light traveled. Since the late seventeenth century, there had been two theories about light: one insisted light was made of waves, and the other said that light was made of particles.

Young was determined to find out which theory was correct. He saw that when two waves of water collided, they either joined together to make a bigger wave or they stopped moving and the water evened out. This happened because the trough of one wave hit the crest of the other wave. The waves canceled each other out, and the wave of water disappeared. Young wondered if light behaved in the same way. He designed his famous double-slit experiment where he sent light through a series of screens with small slits cut out and observed the same things he saw in the water. This proved that light moves in transverse waves, just like water.

The resulting pattern of light from Thomas Young's experiment shows light and dark spots. The light spots come from places where the crests of two light waves have met. The dark spots show where the crest of one wave and the trough of another have canceled each other out.

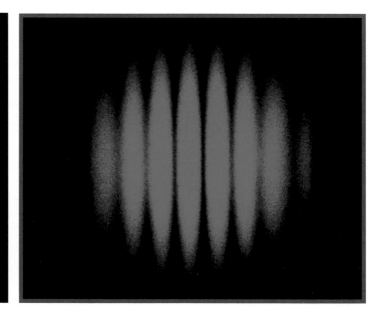

# SCIENCE IN PRACTICE

Sir Isaac Newton thought light was made of particles, but Thomas Young proved that light was a wave. A little more than one hundred years later, physicist Albert Einstein proposed a new hypothesis. He did not dispute Young's theory but noticed that light did not always behave like a wave. Rather, he saw that metal releases particles called electrons when exposed to light. Einstein believed light particles transferred energy to electrons in matter. He determined that light might be both a particle *and* a wave.

Albert Einstein observed that sometimes scientists had to use different theories to explain the behavior of light. He continued to ask questions and form hypotheses until he found an answer that solved the problem of the conflicting information.

# CHAPTER 2

# HOW DOES SOUND TRAVEL?

**H**ave you ever played with a slinky? It bounces and stretches, springing as you move it in your hands. Sound waves move in much the same way.

## A SOUND YOU CANNOT HEAR

Sound waves move differently than light waves, but for a long time, scientists didn't know how or why. A major breakthrough came in 1660 when British scientist Robert Boyle realized

Sound waves bunch up and then spread out, much like a slinky does as it bounces down the stairs.

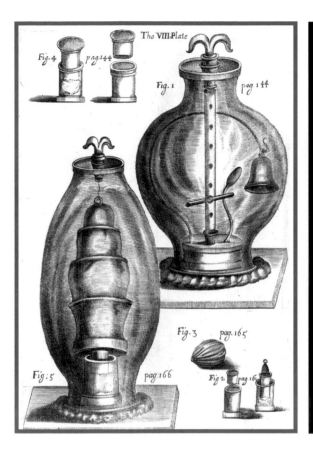

The VIII Plate

Fig. 4 · pag. 144

Fig. 1 · pag. 144

Fig. 3 · pag. 165

Fig. 5 · pag. 166

Fig. 2 · pag. 165

This artwork is from Boyle's work, published in 1669. In the upper right, you can see a depiction of his experiment with the bell in a vacuum jar.

that unlike light waves, sound waves need a material to travel through.

Boyle asked whether sound could travel in a vacuum, a space that does not contain matter such as air. He placed a bell in a glass jar, then used a vacuum pump to remove all the air from the jar. He found that the bell's sound became quieter as the air was removed. Boyle realized that for sound waves to move from their source, they needed to go

Robert Boyle's discovery laid the groundwork for later scientists to add to our understanding of sound waves.

through a **medium**, such as air or water. This was a key breakthrough in understanding sound.

## LONGITUDINAL WAVES

Twenty years later, Newton built upon Boyle's findings to theorize how sound waves work. Newton used math to explain that sound moves in **longitudinal waves**. These waves are made of **pressure**. They **compress** and then stretch out the material to travel. They work like a spring that has been squeezed and then let go. The coils bunch up and then spread out as the energy travels across the spring.

## SOUND WAVES MOVING

Later, scientists discovered that a sound wave pushes the **molecules** in the medium it travels through. These molecules move in the direction of the wave's path. They compress and expand as the waves travel from their source

# TRANSVERSE AND LONGITUDINAL WAVES

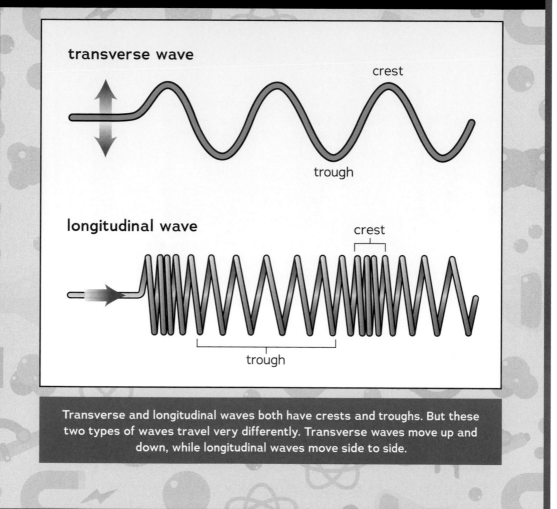

transverse wave

crest

trough

longitudinal wave

crest

trough

Transverse and longitudinal waves both have crests and troughs. But these two types of waves travel very differently. Transverse waves move up and down, while longitudinal waves move side to side.

outward. This makes an area of high pressure—the wave's crest. Then the wave spreads out, which is the wave's trough. Sound waves travel through a medium and into our ear, where our body processes the sound so that we can hear.

Think of when you've heard things through different kinds of materials. What types of mediums do you think allow sound waves to travel the fastest?

The molecules in the medium are important in transferring the sound, but sometimes they can make the sound softer. Waves break down as they are traveling, by losing the energy due to **friction** between the particles in the medium. Some mediums allow the sound waves to experience more friction, and in doing so dampen the sound, more than others.

# CHAPTER 3

# WHERE DO COLORS COME FROM?

**G**o outside on a sunny day, and bright light reveals colors everywhere. But where do these colors come from? As Newton found out, it all starts with the sun.

These leaves look green because of light from the sun.

## NEWTON'S PRISM EXPERIMENT

In the 1670s, Newton was curious about what made up the light from the sun, so he designed an experiment. He used a prism, a glass three-dimensional object with flat sides, to help him see light in a new way. He allowed sunlight to enter a darkened room through a small hole in a window shade. Then he placed the prism in the beam's path in front of a white wall. When the sunlight hit the prism, the light's path bent inside the prism. On the wall beyond it

# NEWTON'S PRISM EXPERIMENT

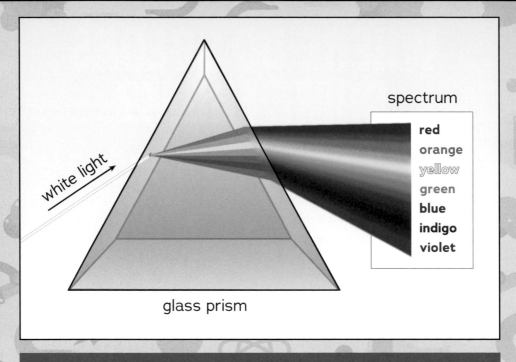

white light

glass prism

spectrum

**red**
**orange**
**yellow**
**green**
**blue**
**indigo**
**violet**

When the white light hit the side of Newton's glass prism in just the right way, it bent and spread out. The process revealed the spectrum of colors that make up the white light that first entered the room.

were the seven colors of the rainbow. Newton called these colors the spectrum. He found that white light is made of many different colors, ranging from very red to very purple and everywhere in between on the spectrum.

The separated colors in Newton's experiment showed that the energy in sunlight contains light waves with different

**wavelengths**—a measure of the distance between a wave's crests or troughs.

Later, scientists found that some colors move differently than others. Some colors have more wavelengths during a given amount of time. This measurement of wavelength over time is called **frequency**. In Newton's experiment, different frequencies of light waves bent at slightly different angles in the prism. This separated the light into its different colors. One last measure of light waves, the height of the crest, or **amplitude**, tells you how intense or bright the light will be.

A rainbow is made up of tiny water drops. When light enters the water, it bends, just as it did when it entered Newton's prism. The combination of the light and water shows the rainbow of colors you see across the sky.

# PARTS OF A TRANSVERSE WAVE

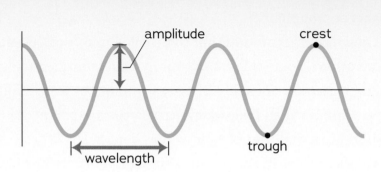

amplitude  crest

wavelength

trough

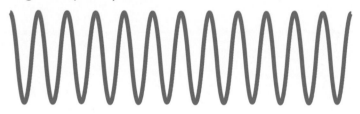

high-frequency wave

low-frequency wave

The properties of a transverse wave tell us a lot about what we will expect from that form of light. You can determine how bright the light will be and what color you might see.

# VISIBLE LIGHT

Newton's experiment revealed the rainbow of colors within visible light. We see those colors in objects around us, which absorb and reflect different wavelengths in light. If a plant looks green, that's because it has absorbed all the sunlight's colors except for green. It reflects the green-colored wavelength, so the plant looks green to us.

This visible light is just one part of the energy that comes from the sun. The sun radiates much more energy that we cannot see. The entire spectrum of its energy is called **electromagnetic radiation**. The electromagnetic spectrum includes everything from the light we can see to the waves that travel to our radios.

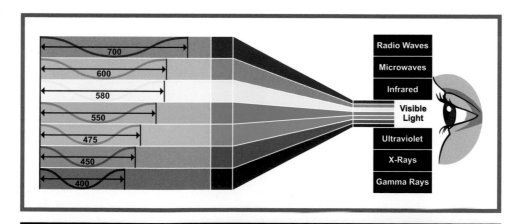

Different forms of energy in electromagnetic radiation have different wavelengths. The human eye can only see the range of wavelengths in what we call visible light. But humans also use other forms of electromagnetic radiation, such as microwaves and X-rays.

# CHAPTER 4

# WHAT MAKES DIFFERENT SOUNDS?

There are many different sounds in the world, from the deep bass at a rock concert to the high chirp of a bird. But what makes these sounds different? You can understand how we hear different kinds of sounds by looking at an acoustic guitar. As a player strums the strings, the guitar makes some notes that are deeper and some that are higher. The vibrating strings produce sound waves that travel out from the guitar by vibrating and compressing the air around the strings.

A guitar player can make strings shorter or longer by pressing down on them. This makes the guitar produce different notes.

Galileo Galilei's experiments laid the groundwork for our current understanding of the frequencies of sound waves.

## A SOUND'S PITCH

Just like light waves, sound waves have different wavelengths. The shorter their wavelengths are, the higher the sound's frequency and the higher the pitch. Italian scientist Galileo Galilei noticed this in the 1630s. He investigated the sounds made when he scraped a chisel across a brass plate. A fast scrape made more lines in the plate and a higher sound, while a slower scrape produced fewer lines and a lower sound. Galileo compared the scrapes to frequencies of a sound wave. We now know that high frequencies make high-pitched notes, while lower frequencies make low-pitched notes.

# ❓ ECHOLOCATION

Bats fly at night without bumping into trees or buildings. How do they do it? A bat's sense of direction is all due to sound waves! First, a bat sends out sounds from its mouth or nose, in frequencies too high for humans to hear. The longitudinal sound waves travel for as long as they can, compressing the air as they go. When the sound waves hit something solid, the waves bounce back in an echo. Bats have extremely sensitive hearing and can tell where something is by its echo. If it's food, they know just where to find their next meal.

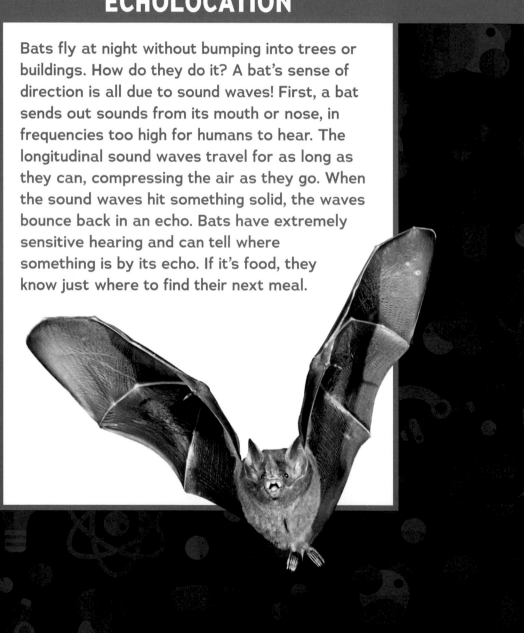

Think of your favorite song. Can you pick out sound waves with different properties? When does the sound have a higher amplitude or pitch? What has happened to the sound wave?

## WHAT MAKES A SOUND LOUDER?

Some sound waves have a higher amplitude than others. If a guitar player strums the strings really hard, the sound is loud. The sound wave has a bigger vibration and can be heard more clearly from farther away than the notes that have been played more softly. This is the sound's amplitude. Your ears hear the pitch and loudness of notes in a song. If you know about sound waves, you know what features make these things happen.

# CHAPTER 5

# WHAT HAPPENS TO A SIREN'S SOUND?

**H**ave you ever been on the street and heard an ambulance coming? As it gets closer, the pitch of the siren gets higher and louder. The sound is loudest when the ambulance is right by you. Then it passes you, and the sound changes. It not only gets quieter, but the sound is different—it has a lower pitch. What makes the sound change?

Scientists heard the changing pitch of moving things long before we had modern vehicles like ambulances.

## UNDERSTANDING MOVING SOUNDS

You hear the sound change as the ambulance zooms past because you're standing still while the sound is moving. Inside the ambulance, the sound is the same, but the speeding vehicle makes the frequency of the waves that you hear change.

When the ambulance heads toward you, the siren's sound waves are shortened and faster because of the added speed of the moving ambulance. Short wavelengths make higher sounds. When the ambulance passes you, you are behind the sound's source. You are hearing the change in frequency as the ambulance moves away from you. The sound waves have a lower frequency, making a lower sound. This is called the Doppler effect.

Austrian physicist Christian Doppler first described the Doppler effect in 1842, but he focused on light from stars rather than sounds. Because light and sound both travel in waves, the Doppler effect applies to both kinds of energy.

# SCIENCE IN PRACTICE

In 1845 Dutch meteorologist Christophorus Buys Ballot (*below*) conducted an experiment using a train and trumpet players. He hired a train to carry trumpeters who played a constant note of G. It passed three trumpeters on the ground also playing G. There weren't any devices to measure a change in the note, so Buys Ballot used human ears to measure the change. After two days of experiments, the results showed that the sound's pitch on the train was lower as it moved away. This proved the Doppler effect for sound.

With so many sources of sound and light in this world,
there is plenty more to explore.

## SOUND AND LIGHT EVERYWHERE

From guitar notes to a star's distant light, sound and light
move in waves. Scientists have studied how sound and light
waves work. Their experiments, research, and results help
us understand how this energy moves and what it contains.
With further scientific inquiry, maybe we can all understand
a bit more about the mysteries of light and sound.

# TRY IT!

You've learned that sound waves move through matter. Do you think the sounds change when moving through different kinds of matter? Try this experiment to find out how sound moves through a gas, a solid, and a liquid.

## ❷ WHAT YOU'LL NEED

- three sealable plastic sandwich bags
- water
- sugar
- table
- coin
- notebook
- pen

## ❷ WHAT YOU'LL DO

1. Fill a bag halfway with water. Squeeze out the extra air. Seal the bag.
2. Fill a second bag halfway with sugar. Squeeze out the extra air. Seal the bag.
3. Blow some air into the third bag. Then seal it.

4. Put the bag with water on a table. Place your ear on the bag. Tap on the table with the coin, and listen for a sound. Write down what you observe about the sound.
5. Put the bag with sugar on the table. Place your ear on the bag. Tap the coin on the table, and record your observations about the sound.
6. Try it with the bag of air. Write down what you hear.

## ❷ FOLLOW-UP

Review your recorded data. Compare the results of the sounds you heard through the different bags. Which medium made the sound seem loudest? Did any of the mediums muffle the sound? What can you conclude about sound waves moving through matter from your results?

# GLOSSARY

**amplitude:** a measurement of the movement or vibration of something, such as a wave. A wave's amplitude is the height of the wave.

**compress:** compression is the reduction of the volume of something by the application of force or pressure

**electromagnetic radiation:** energy from sunlight that moves in waves

**frequency:** the number of wavelengths that move past a certain point over a set period of time

**friction:** a rubbing force that slows down objects

**longitudinal wave:** a wave with vibrating particles of a medium that move in the direction of the wave

**medium:** a substance through which something acts or is moved

**molecule:** the smallest part of a substance that displays all the chemical properties of that substance; made up of more than one atom

**pressure:** the force made by pressing on something

**transverse wave:** a wave in which the vibrating part of the wave moves perpendicular to the direction of the wave

**wavelength:** the distance between two consecutive wave crest peaks or the lowest points of consecutive troughs

# FURTHER INFORMATION

American Museum of Natural History: Einstein
http://www.amnh.org/exhibitions/einstein/

BBC Earth: What Is a Ray of Light Made Of?
http://www.bbc.com/earth/story/20150731-what-is-a-ray-of-light
-made-of

Johnson, Robin. *The Science of Sound Waves*. New York:
Crabtree, 2017.

KidsHealth: Your Ears
http://kidshealth.org/en/kids/ears.html

National Oceanic and Atmospheric Administration: How Far Does
Sound Travel in the Ocean?
http://oceanservice.noaa.gov/facts/sound.html

Oxlade, Chris. *Experiments with Sound and Light*. New York:
PowerKids, 2015.

Rowell, Rebecca. *Energy and Waves through Infographics*.
Minneapolis: Lerner Publications, 2014.

Yasuda, Anita. *Explore Light and Optics! With 25 Great Projects*.
White River Junction, VT: Nomad, 2016.

# INDEX

# PHOTO ACKNOWLEDGMENTS

The images in this book are used with the permission of: design elements: © iStockphoto.com/kotoffei; iDesign/Shutterstock.com. Nikola Spasenoski/ Shutterstock.com, p. 4; Mat Hayward/Shutterstock.com, p. 5; © Paparazzofamily/ Dreamstime.com, p. 6; Veter Sergey/Shutterstock.com, p. 7; © GIPhotoStock/ Science Source, p. 8; World History Archive/Alamy Stock Photo, p. 9; © Newlight/ Dreamstime.com, p. 10; © Wellcome Images/Science Source, p. 11; 19th era/Alamy Stock Photo, p. 12; © Laura Westlund/Independent Picture Service, pp. 13, 16, 18; kurhan/Shutterstock.com, p. 14; liam1949/Shutterstock.com, p. 15; Daniel Schreiber/ Shutterstock.com, p. 17; udaix/Shutterstock.com, p. 19; © Hugo Maes/Dreamstime. com, p. 20; Georgios Kollidas/Shutterstock.com, p. 21; Ivan Kuzmin/Shutterstock. com, p. 22; Alexmama/Shutterstock.com, p. 23; Peter Titmuss/Shutterstock.com, p. 24; © Imagno/Hulton Archive/Getty Images, p. 25; Wikimedia Commons (public domain), p. 26; Andrey Prokhorov/Shutterstock.com, p. 27.

Front cover: © iStockphoto.com/teekid.